Novels for Students, Volume 39

Project Editor: Sara Constantakis Rights Acquisition and Management: Margaret Chamberlain-Gaston, Jacqueline Flowers Composition: Evi Abou-El-Seoud Manufacturing: Rhonda Dover

Imaging: John Watkins

Product Design: Pamela A. E. Galbreath, Jennifer Wahi Content Conversion: Katrina Coach Product Manager: Meggin Condino © 2012 Gale, Cengage Learning

For product information and technology assistance, contact us at **Gale Customer Support, 1-800-877-4253**.

For permission to use material from this text or product, submit all requests online at **www.cengage.com/permissions**.

Further permissions questions can be emailed to **permissionrequest@cengage.com** While every effort has been made to ensure the reliability of the information presented in this publication, Gale, a part of Cengage Learning, does not guarantee the accuracy of the data contained herein. Gale accepts no payment for listing; and inclusion in the publication of any organization, agency, institution, publication, service, or individual does not imply endorsement of the editors or publisher. Errors brought to the attention of the publisher and verified to the satisfaction of the publisher will be corrected in future editions.

Gale 27500 Drake Rd.
Farmington Hills, MI, 48331-3535

ISBN-13: 978-1-4144-6702-3
ISBN-10: 1-4144-6702-8
ISSN 1094-3552

This title is also available as an e-book.

ISBN-13: 978-1-4144-7368-0
ISBN-10: 1-4144-7368-0
Contact your Gale, a part of Cengage Learning sales representative for ordering information.

Printed in Mexico
1 2 3 4 5 6 7 16 15 14 13 12

Oryx and Crake

Margaret Atwood

2003

Introduction

Canadian writer Margaret Atwood's 2003 novel *Oryx and Crake* paints a terrifying picture of a not-so-distant future in which genetic engineering runs amok and all of human civilization lies in ruins, the victim of a deadly viral plague. Although some classify the novel as science fiction, Atwood prefers the term *speculative fiction,* as this term suggests that the story is rooted in ideas, concepts, and events already present in contemporary society. Indeed, the advances in bioengineering in years since the novel's publication eerily parallel some of the events in the story.

Atwood reveals, in an essay she wrote for *PMLA*, that she began the novel while on a trip to Australia, "the land of dreamtime." She continues, "I 'saw' the book as I was looking over a balcony at a rare red-headed crake, during a birding expedition."

Like many of Atwood's earlier novels, *Oryx and Crake* has been popular with both critics and general readers. It was shortlisted for the Man Booker Prize in 2003 and was also named a *New York Times* Notable Book.

Oryx and Crake is not a book for children; readers should be aware that there are many troubling scenes depicting violence, drug use, pornography, and sex. In addition, the postapocalyptic setting is frightening. For the more mature reader, however, *Oryx and Crake* offers not only a look toward a horrifying future but also a biting satire of contemporary society, a heartbreaking romance, and an exciting quest story.

Author Biography

Atwood was born on November 18, 1939, in Ottawa, Ontario, Canada, to Margaret and Carl Atwood. Her father was an entomologist who conducted research in the bush country of northern Ontario and Quebec. Consequently, Atwood and her brother spent every summer camping in the far north, returning to Toronto each year for the school year. (Her younger sister was not born until 1951.) During this time, she accompanied her father in the field, but she also spent a great deal of time reading.

Atwood began writing seriously when she was sixteen. She attended Victoria College of the University of Toronto beginning in 1957; there, she earned an arts degree with honors in English. She published her first book of poetry, *Double Persephone*, in 1961, the year she graduated. Next, she attended Radcliffe College, which is associated with Harvard University, on a graduate fellowship and completed a master of arts degree in English. She began Ph.D. studies at Harvard but did not complete the degree and returned to Canada. She spent the next ten years teaching English at a variety of Canadian universities. In 1967, she married James Polk, an American. However, the marriage did not last, and the couple separated in 1972 and divorced in 1977. Atwood established a long-term relationship with the Canadian novelist Graeme Gibson in 1972, and the couple remains together. They have one daughter.

The 1970s were good years for Atwood creatively; she published three novels (including *Surfacing* in 1972), a book of short stories, and five volumes of poetry. She also wrote the benchmark critical survey of Canadian literature, *Survival: A Thematic Guide to Canadian Literature*, in 1972. In 1980, Atwood and her family moved to Toronto, where they have remained ever since.

Throughout the next decades, Atwood proved herself to be an amazingly prolific writer, producing many well-received critical works, including novels, volumes of short stories, books of poetry, children's books, and essays. Atwood's Web site lists seventeen volumes of poetry, seven collections of short stories, thirteen novels, seven children's books, and nine book-length collections of criticism. She has also edited six books, written a play, and published a number of special editions for small presses.

Although Atwood has been well known as a writer since the 1970s, her 1985 novel *The Handmaid's Tale* was her breakout success, winning her global readership. The novel was shortlisted for the Booker Prize, and it won the Arthur C. Clarke award in 1987 for best science fiction novel and the *Los Angeles Times* fiction award. In addition, the book was wildly popular with readers, appearing on the *New York Times* best-seller list for fifteen weeks in the hardcover edition. In 1987, when the novel was released in paperback, it again appeared on the *New York Times* list, this time for eight weeks. When the movie version of the novel appeared in

1990, the novel once more hit the best-seller lists. In 2000, the novel *Blind Assassin* won the Booker Prize.

In 2003, Atwood returned to speculative fiction with the publication of *Oryx and Crake*, a dystopic novel that describes a near-future global catastrophe. In 2009, Atwood published *Year of the Flood*. The setting of this novel is contemporary with *Oryx and Crake*, and some of the same characters appear in both.

Atwood's work has been translated into more than forty languages, according to her Web site. She is far and away the most honored and recognized writer in Canada. Moreover, she is acknowledged internationally as one of the most important writers of the twentieth and twenty-first centuries.

Plot Summary

Oryx and Crake is narrated by a character called Snowman who tells the story both in the present and in flashback, when, as a child and young man, he was known as Jimmy. The book opens in a strange and forbidding setting, and the reader must piece together both the past and the present to make sense of the story. In this summary, the name "Snowman" is used to indicate the present time in the novel, while the name "Jimmy" refers to events in flashback.

Chapter 1

The first chapter introduces Snowman as he awakens, somewhere near a seacoast. There are reefs made of destroyed cars and buildings; as the scene unfolds, it becomes clear that the setting is postapocalyptic and that the story is told in some unspecified future time after a huge catastrophe. Even on the first page, the tone is grim: Snowman is terrified, he is covered in bites and scabs, there is little food, and his only clothing is a dirty bed sheet and a Red Sox baseball hat.

In the next scene, Snowman watches some children on the beach. These children and their parents are the Children of Crake, also called Crakers—beautiful, genetically engineered to withstand the sun's dangerous ultraviolet light and viral diseases. Snowman appears to be the only human being who has survived the catastrophe, and he is barely surviving. The Children of Crake treat Snowman as if he is a god or an oracle, someone who can teach them about the world. Although the names Crake and Oryx are referenced, little is revealed, other than that Snowman seems to blame Crake for the current situation, and he hears Oryx's voice in his mind.

Media Adaptations

- In 2003, Random House produced *Oryx and Crake* as an unabridged, downloadable audiobook, narrated by Campbell Scott.

Chapter 2

The second chapter is a flashback to Snowman's childhood, to when he was a boy named

Jimmy. In the flashback, Jimmy's father works as a genographer, or someone who maps genes, at OrganInc Farms, a place where scientists genetically engineer animals to serve as hosts for organs that can be transplanted into humans. Pigoons, for example, are pig derivatives that have been developed to grow five or six kidneys.

One of Jimmy's earliest memories is watching a huge bonfire of cows, sheep, and pigs that were infected by disease; there is some indication that humans caused the animals to become infected. The incident foreshadows later events in the novel.

Jimmy, his mother, and his father live at the OrganInc compound, a sealed community. Jimmy attends OrganInc School. Outside the compound are the pleeblands, inhabited by violent and unpredictable poor people. Jimmy's mother and father are growing increasingly estranged. Once a microbiologist for OrganInc, she now stays at home all day, growing ever more depressed.

Chapter 3

The story returns to the present. Snowman has problems with the heat, humidity, and intense sun. Severe storms occur as well, and although the setting is vaguely on the eastern coast of North America, the daily afternoon thunderstorms suggest a tropical climate. The implication is that these are the products of global warming. There are references to Snowman's early days in this strange new world and information about the other creatures that share the world with Snowman. The pigoons have become feral and dangerous. Wolvogs, a genetically engineered cross between a wolf and a dog, also roam in packs.

Chapter 4

In a flashback, Snowman recalls his tenth birthday, when his father gives him a rakunk. The rakunk is a cross between a skunk and a raccoon, developed as part of a "Create an Animal" game played among the geneticists. Jimmy calls him Killer.

Jimmy's father gets a new job at HelthWyzer, and the family moves to a new compound where the security is even stricter than at OrganInc. Jimmy's mother grows more and more despondent and says she feels like a prisoner. She is opposed to the research Jimmy's father is doing. Meanwhile, fanatics storm the HelthWyzer gates with spray bottles of highly dangerous infectious diseases.

Jimmy's mother finally leaves the family. She destroys her computer and her husband's computer before she leaves. It is unclear whether she does this in revenge or as a security precaution. She also takes Jimmy's pet rakunk with her; in a note to Jimmy, she says that she will "liberate" the creature. Jimmy is bereft and angry. Jimmy and his father are questioned by men from CorpSeCorps, or corporate security corps, a quasi-police agency that wields tremendous power.

Meanwhile, Jimmy has met a student named

Glenn, who later assumes the name of Crake. Jimmy's teacher asks him to show Crake around the school. Crake is brilliant and quickly moves to the top of the class. He and Jimmy become close friends and spend all of their time outside of school together, usually playing computer simulation games. Their favorite is Extinctathon, a game in which the player has to identify bioforms that have gone extinct within the previous fifty years.

The two boys also surf the Internet, visiting pornography sites by using a password belonging to Crake's mother's boyfriend. They also smoke his marijuana while they play on the computer. It is while they are surfing the Internet that they run across a child porn site and are both entranced by a small girl. In the flashback, Snowman refers to the girl as Oryx, although it is unclear whether the child they see on the porn site is really the same person as the woman they later know as Oryx.

At the end of the chapter, Snowman flashes back to a time after Jimmy's childhood and adolescence, a time when, as adults, Jimmy and Oryx become lovers.

Chapter 5

In a return to the present, Snowman recalls how he began teaching the Crakers in the days immediately after the catastrophe. He tells them that Crake created them and Oryx continues to provide for them. One of the "laws" he hands down to them is that the genetically engineered rabbits that dot the countryside are sacred to Oryx and must not be eaten. He also specifies that the Crakers must catch and grill a fish once a week and bring it to him to eat.

In this chapter, readers learn more about the Crakers: they are vegetarian, their skin tones range from very white to black, they have green eyes, and they are all beautiful. They ask Snowman to explain the things they find on the beach, the remains of a human civilization that has gone extinct. Snowman finds himself making up answers for them, and it seems that the Crakers are developing a religion that centers around Oryx and Crake.

Snowman gives into his desolation and searches out a bottle of Scotch whiskey he has been saving. He drinks it all and howls at the moon. Soon, wolvogs surround the base of the tree where he sleeps. He tosses the bottle at them and they scatter, but he knows it is only a matter of time before they hunt and kill him. His mind returns to Oryx; he seems to miss her presence more than anything else.

Chapter 6

Snowman recounts the story of Oryx, as she told it to him when they were lovers. As a child living in a developing nation, Oryx was a member of large and desperately poor family living in a remote village. A man called Uncle En periodically visited villages like this one, offering to buy children and take them to the city, where they could earn money. Oryx and her brother were sold.

They were taken to a tiny room in a city inhabited by many children. Oryx was instructed to sell flowers in the street until a man asked her to come up to his room. Once there, he told her to take off her dress. Uncle En burst into the room and extorted money from the man.

Later, another man took charge of the children, and Oryx learned that Uncle En had been murdered. Her new job was to act in pornographic movies like the one that Crake and Jimmy watched on their computer. As Oryx tells Jimmy about her life, he becomes very angry and protective of her. Oryx, on the other hand, is very matter-of-fact about what has happened to her.

Chapter 7

Snowman awakens from his drinking binge on the platform in the tree where he lives. He knows that he must find some food. Retrieving his remaining food from a hiding place, he realizes that he does not have enough to sustain himself in the long run. If he can kill a pigoon, he thinks, he will have plenty of food. But the pigoons are very smart and violent, and he has no weapons. He decides he must travel to the RejoovenEsense Compound to gather supplies and guns. The RejoovenEsense Compound is where he lived with Crake and Oryx before the catastrophe. Crake built a bubble dome called Paradice where the Crakers were created.

Snowman goes to the Crakers' village to tell

them he will be gone for a few days. He finds the men performing their morning ritual of urinating around the perimeter of their settlement. Crake has genetically engineered them to give off chemicals in their urine that act as a repellent to creatures such as wolvogs, bobkittens, pigoons, and rakunks.

He also observes the women engaging in purring, a practice that involves sound waves in healing. One of the children has been attacked by a bobkitten, and the women purr over him. He also notes that the Crakers grow very quickly, reaching adolescence by four years old. At age thirty, they die.

Snowman tells the Crakers he is going to see Crake. They want to come along, but he forbids it. Snowman starts out on the long journey.

Chapter 8

While walking toward the compound, Snowman flashes back to the day when he and Crake graduated from HelthWyzer High. Crake finished at the top of his class and was invited to attend Watson-Crick Institute, while Jimmy was accepted only at the very low ranking Martha Graham Academy. At their graduation party, Crake tells Jimmy that his mother has died, the victim of a horrible virus that dissolved her flesh. Crake's father died some time before, the result of falling off a highway overpass.

Soon after, large numbers of people begin protesting the Happicuppa coffee bean, devised by

HelthWyzer. This bean could be harvested with machines. While watching the protests on television, Jimmy sees his mother as part of a shouting crowd rushing CorpSeCorps men. He fears for her safety.

Later, the boys go their separate ways. The Martha Graham Academy is an underfunded, deteriorating institution. Once a school where students studied fine arts, most students at Martha Graham now studied graphics arts and writing designed for advertising, marketing, and propaganda. As a Martha Graham student, Jimmy is not challenged intellectually, and he spends most of his time chasing girls.

Crake, on the other hand, is at the prestigious Watson-Crick Institute, where students study mathematics and science. He invites Jimmy to visit him over Thanksgiving, and Jimmy accepts. Once there, Jimmy is again interrogated by CorpSeCorps men concerning his mother.

Crake takes Jimmy on a tour of the campus and shows him the new products that students are working on, including something called "ChickieNobs." These are genetically engineered chickens that have no beaks, brains, or eyes, but they have extra legs, thighs, and breasts. The chickens are headed for the fast-food industry.

Crake also confides in Jimmy that his father's death was not an accident. He suspects that CorpSeCorps had him murdered because he knew that HelthWyzer was not only creating cures for disease but also creating diseases so that they could sell the cures.

Later, Crake reveals that he has become a grandmaster in Extinctathon and that "playrooms" on the site are filled with leaked documents from CorpSeCorps. It becomes clear that the inner workings of Extinctathon are being run by anti-corporation activists known collectively as MaddAddam.

Chapter 9

This chapter flashes to the present, with Snowman walking through the pleeblands. He finally reaches the RejoovenEsense Compound and tries to find food in a house. The inhabitants of the house are dead; the husband's body is still in the bathtub, and the wife's body is in the bedroom. There is a child's room and pictures of the family, but the child is not in the house. Snowman steals some supplies and then leaves the house, only to find a group of pigoons watching him. Snowman is able to scare them off, but just barely. He knows they will return.

Suddenly, a huge storm approaches. He slips into one of the gatehouses next to the security building. The lights come on, and he sees dead bodies in biosuits. He moves to the interior of the building, sits, and starts to drink the alcohol he found in the house.

Chapter 10

Snowman flashes back to his graduation from Martha Graham. He moves in with his girlfriend and her roommates, who are all artists. However, the relationship sours and ends when Jimmy takes a job with AnooYoo, a minor corporate compound.

Jimmy moves to AnooYoo and cuts off all communication with his father and his second wife. He receives a promotion and begins buying electronics and other consumer goods. In addition, he has a series of affairs with married women who are only looking for a little excitement. Neither Jimmy nor the women want commitment of any sort.

Meanwhile, Crake is working at RejoovenEsense, one of the top compounds. He and Jimmy have some communication, and Crake tells Jimmy that his mother's boyfriend has died suddenly, with a virus. The implication is that Crake has maneuvered to make this happen.

While watching the news, Jimmy becomes aware of a wave of young girls found locked in garages. The girls have been forced to engage in the sex trade and pornography. One young woman is interviewed on the television, and Jimmy recognizes her as the child he and Crake saw on the Internet some ten years earlier. It is the woman he will come to know as Oryx.

The CorpSeCorps men begin interrogating him about his mother again. They show him a blindfolded prisoner about to be executed for treason. Just before she is shot, she says, "Goodbye. Remember Killer. I love you. Don't let me down." He realizes that she is his mother. After this encounter, he enters a deep depression and realizes that the work he has been doing at AnooYoo is meaningless. What he wants is revenge.

Chapter 11

Snowman, hiding in the gatehouse, is awakened from a dream by the sound of a land crab digging through the wall. As he leaves the gatehouse, he sees a group of pigoons charging him. He runs back to the gatehouse, but the pigoons follow him in. He runs upstairs, since pigoons have not yet learned to climb. However, he knows it is only a matter of time until they learn how to manage the stairs.

Trapped upstairs, he looks through the supplies that are left in the guardhouse. He finds a radio and hears another human voice speaking in a foreign language. He tries to reply but is unsuccessful.

Earlier, he cut his foot, and now he tends to the cut. There are many viruses and bacteria loose, and he could develop a fatal infection. When night falls, he finds a bed in the gatehouse. He has a troubled night's sleep filled with dreams of his mother.

In the morning, he resupplies himself and makes a plan to escape the guardhouse through the air vents. He is still intent on making it to Paradice.

Once outside, he sees smoke rising from the general direction of the Crakers' encampment. Not knowing what he is facing, he feels an even greater need to acquire weapons from Paradice.

Chapter 12

Snowman pushes on, the heat and his throbbing foot slowing him down. He flashes back to his last days at AnooYoo. Unexpectedly, Crake shows up and offers him a job at RejoovenEsense. Jimmy accepts and finds himself living in great luxury. Crake tells him about a pill called BlyssPluss. The pill will wipe out all sexually transmitted diseases, improve sexual performance, and prolong youth. Jimmy's job will be to handle the advertising campaign.

Jimmy soon gets his first glimpse of Paradice. It is a dome in the RejoovenEsense Compound. It is highly guarded, and only Crake and those he vouches for are allowed to enter. The dome has airlocks so that it can be completely sealed off in the event of terrorism or unexpected plague. Jimmy discovers that the people working on gene splicing in Paradice were all members of MaddAddam. Although they are anti-Compound, Crake has coerced them into coming to work for him.

Crake then shows Jimmy his life's work, the Crakers. Later, when Jimmy looks through the one-way glass into the place where the Crakers live, he sees Oryx. Crake explains that Oryx is their teacher. Crake has found her through a service that provides prostitutes to students at Watson-Crick. He is in love with her.

However, Jimmy is in love with her too. He begins an affair with her and tries to convince her to run away with him. Both Crake and Oryx, at different times, ask Jimmy to take care of the Crakers if anything should happen to them.

One evening, Oryx runs out for a pizza, and while she is gone, an epidemic of a fatal virus breaks out in Brazil. Because Crake is away from the compound and Jimmy is next in charge, he monitors the outbreak. Suddenly, the outbreaks are everywhere throughout the world. He is racked with anxiety over Oryx's location. Finally she calls, crying. She tells him that the virus was in the BlyssPluss pills she has been taking all over the world.

By midnight, it is clear that this is a major catastrophe. The next morning, Oryx and Crake return, and stand at the airlock waiting for Jimmy to let them in. Jimmy refuses, but Crake tells him that he has immunized Jimmy against the virus.

Jimmy opens the airlocks, and Crake staggers in with Oryx, who has passed out. He looks at Jimmy, and says, "I'm counting on you." Then Crake slits Oryx's throat. Jimmy shoots him.

Chapter 13

Snowman walks around Paradice, his foot throbbing. He finds some antibiotics and injects himself. Then, he flashes back to the days immediately after the catastrophe and Oryx and Crake's deaths. He spends hours watching the Crakers, finally introducing himself to them as Snowman. He tells them that Oryx and Crake have left, and that Snowman must take them to a new place. Jimmy leads them out of Paradice, stepping over the bodies of Oryx and Crake. He shoots any infected humans who try to approach them.

Chapter 14

Snowman makes it back to the beach, the infection in his foot growing worse. The Crakers are singing his name in an attempt to lead him back to them. They tell him that they have been visited by two men and a woman while he was gone and that they had guns. Snowman promises to visit the people the next day.

Chapter 15

Snowman wakes early, before sunrise. He is frightened by the thought of confronting the other humans. He does not know whether to try to talk to them or kill them. He fears that if he does not kill them, they will kill him and then kill the Crakers. Yet he does not want to do so. The last words of the book are ambiguous: "From habit he lifts his watch; it shows him its blank face. Zero hour, Snowman thinks. Time to go."

Characters

Crake

Crake is the name assumed by a green-eyed boy originally known as Glenn. He takes this name when he and his friend Jimmy play the Web-based computer game Extinctathon. The red-necked crake is a bird found in New Guinea and Australia. A secretive bird, it is rarely seen by observers. Likewise, throughout the novel, Crake is a secretive character who reveals little about himself.

Crake (then called Glenn) arrives at the HelthWyzer school after his father dies and while his mother is living with her boyfriend, a man Crake calls Uncle Pete. Their teacher asks Jimmy to show Glenn around the school, and the two become fast friends, spending most of their out-of-school time together smoking Uncle Pete's dope and surfing the Internet. They use Uncle Pete's password to access seedy pornography sites. Crake is very adept at hacking into sites and creating computer labyrinths to hide their viewing history and the use of the password. At one point, Crake and Jimmy stumble into a child porn site and see a girl they come to know as Oryx.

Crake is particularly taken with the game Extinctathon, a game that requires an impressive knowledge of extinct creatures. The webmaster of the site is an entity known as MaddAddam. Years after they leave high school, Crake reveals to Jimmy that he has become a grandmaster at the game, and in so doing, has entered the world of MaddAddam, a disruptive, anti-Compound collective of computer hackers and scientists.

While still in high school, Crake proves himself to be a particularly brilliant but cynical young man. He is recruited to attend the Watson-Crick Institute, an elite and powerful university. At Watson-Crick, he lives a life of luxury and begins his studies of gene splicing. Unbeknownst to Jimmy, Crake has Student Services secure for him a young female prostitute while he is in college; he feels sure that she is the girl they saw years before on the Internet. He names her Oryx. After graduation, Crake receives a job at RejoovenEsense, one of the most powerful of all the compounds, taking Oryx with him.

At RejoovenEsense, Crake works on a product known as BlyssPluss, a pill that will increase sexual prowess, eliminate sexually transmitted diseases, and lengthen life span. He hires Jimmy to manage the ad campaign.

Crake's success with this project gives him a great deal of power. As always, he is very secretive about a project of his own design in a dome he calls Paradice. He coerces the top minds of MaddAddam to join his project. (It is implied that he has eliminated the other scientists working in MaddAddam, a clue to his ruthless, secretive nature.)

The project is to genetically engineer a race of humanoids who have all the qualities Crake believes are important for their survival. They are immune to disease, their reproduction is carefully controlled, and they mature early and die upon turning thirty. In creating these beings, Crake reveals his own hubris (pride): all of the creatures have his green eyes, though they have many different colors of skin. In addition, Crake's hubris persuades him that he knows what qualities make up a "perfect" life form.

When Crake shows the project to Jimmy, he reveals that he has Oryx working with the Crakers, as the creatures are called. He also implies that he is in love with her.

As secretive as he is, there are clues to the vengeful nature of Crake's personality. He reveals that his father's death was not an accident but rather the work of the CorpSeCorps men, who did not want his father to reveal that HelthWyzer not only produces diseases as well as their cures. Crake's ultimate vengeance on the human race may be a punishment for his father's death. Likewise, although it is not stated explicitly, there are hints that the disease that kills his mother and Uncle Pete was his creation, a trial run of the disease he would use to destroy the entire human race. Again, this punishment may have been revenge for what he viewed as his mother's betrayal of his father. Finally, Crake kills Oryx in front of Jimmy, an act that could be considered punishment for their affair.

Crake's Father

Crake's father is dead before Jimmy and Crake meet, the supposed victim of an accident in which he fell off a bridge. Crake, however, knows that he was murdered. Crake's father knew that the HelthWyzer Compound produced both cures for diseases and the diseases themselves, in order to turn a profit. That knowledge cost him his life.

Crake's Mother

Crake's mother is a shadowy figure who ends up dissolving because of a terrible disease. Clues in the story suggest that she knew that her husband knew about HelthWyzer Compound's creation of diseases and informs on him to the CorpSeCorps. She and Crake move in with her boyfriend shortly after her husband's death.

Glenn

See Crake

Jimmy

See Snowman

Jimmy's Father

Jimmy's father is a genographer, a scientist who maps gene sequences. He is very good at his job and is hired by an important biogenetic firm known as HelthWyzer. Although he believes that the work he does is for the benefit of humanity, there are times when he seems to know that he has morally sold out in order to obtain a good lifestyle.

After his wife leaves, Jimmy's father begins an affair with his laboratory assistant, who eventually moves into the house. He seems oblivious to the needs of his child, Jimmy.

Jimmy's Mother

Jimmy's mother is a bioscientist who previously worked for the OrganFarm Compound. After Jimmy is born, she spends more time at home, eventually not working at all. She is despondent about her condition and grows increasingly agitated by the work her husband is doing. She believes that the genetic work he is doing is against nature and is morally wrong. Eventually, she escapes from the compound, destroying her and her husband's computers as she leaves. She also takes Jimmy's rakunk with her, leaving a note that tells Jimmy that she will "liberate" the animal.

She continues to send unsigned postcards to Jimmy throughout the story. Jimmy sees her participating in a protest against a HelthWyzer product, and later sees a video of her execution as a traitor.

Jimmy's mother may have followed her moral compass in leaving the HelthWyzer Compound, but in so doing, she left her son to fend for himself. She emerges as an essentially selfish person, despite her willingness to fight for what she believes in. Her absence and her choice to put protest before motherhood mark Jimmy deeply.

Oryx

Oryx is a young woman originally from a developing country. Her family, desperately poor, has sold her to a man who wants her to sell flowers in the city at first, but who really wants to engage her in the child sex trade. Later, she is sold to another man who has her act in pornographic movies. Finally, she meets Crake when she comes to him as a prostitute. He is in love with her, and he hires her as part of a special project.

Of the three main characters in *Oryx and Crake*, Oryx is the greatest mystery. She tells the details of her life to Jimmy in a very matter-of-fact manner and never dwells on the terrible conditions under which she has had to live. She seems to understand her own sexuality, even as a child, as a commodity to be bought and sold.

While Jimmy agonizes over her past, Oryx wants to leave it behind. She suggests that the conditions working in the child pornography studio were much better than the conditions in her home village. There is a moment, however, when it is clear that, as a small child, she desperately missed her mother. In the flashback sequences to Oryx's childhood, it is clear that she misses her mother dreadfully.

Like Jimmy, Oryx has been deserted and

betrayed by her mother. Like Jimmy, she does not seem to form close personal bonds. Although she is intimate with both Crake and Jimmy, she shares very little of herself or her emotional life with either of them.

Snowman

Snowman is the narrator of the story, so all its events and characters are filtered through his consciousness. His age is not specified, but through the course of the story, readers learn that he is probably in his thirties. He may be slightly mad; he hears the voice of a woman he loves in his head. He appears to be the sole survivor of a catastrophe that has destroyed the entire human race. He lives in a tree to protect himself from the carnivores that inhabit the landscape. His primary responsibility is to care for the Children of Crake, a genetically engineered race of hominids.

Over the course of the book, Snowman recalls his life as Jimmy (his given name) in flashbacks, ranging from the time he was five years old until the apocalyptic moment when everyone is dying of a viral infection and he shoots Crake.

Jimmy is a lover and collector of archaic words. Just as Crake is fascinated with extinct bioforms, Jimmy is entranced by extinct and dying words.

As a boy, Jimmy is intelligent but underachieving. He is deeply sensitive to his parents' marital problems, and he alternately loves and hates both his mother and his father. As a child, he seems to have had no friends. The only thing he truly loves is the rakunk, a genetically engineered animal that his father gives him for his tenth birthday. The gift, however, causes another rift in his parents' marriage.

When Jimmy's mother ultimate leaves her family, Jimmy feels angry, grief-stricken, and betrayed. Not only has his mother deserted him, she has taken his rakunk with her, leaving him without love. Moreover, when his father begins bringing home his lab assistant, Jimmy feels once more betrayed and unloved.

In high school, Jimmy meets Crake (then called Glenn), and Crake becomes his one true friend. The two spend all of their time together, mostly surfing the Internet. Jimmy is deeply touched when they see a girl on a pornography site, and her image stays with him the rest of his life.

Jimmy is not a good student. Although it seems clear that he is intelligent, he does not apply himself. In addition, his intellectual strength is words, not mathematics or science. Because the arts are so devalued in this society, he finds himself at a run-down, dilapidated university while Crack goes off to the most elite university.

Jimmy does not apply himself in college either and is unable to form lasting relationships with women, although he always has a girlfriend. It is likely that his mother's desertion and the general tone of the society he lives in have made it impossible for him to emotionally commit to anyone.

When he ultimately comes to work with Crake at RejoovenEsense, he discovers Oryx there, and knows that Crake is in love with her. Despite this, he has an affair with Oryx; he is deeply in love with her. This love, however, causes him pain because he is betraying Crake, his one friend.

After Crake kills Oryx in front of Jimmy during the early hours of the massive viral epidemic, Jimmy, without even thinking, shoots Crake and kills him. It is difficult to know whether this is yet another betrayal of Crake, whether it is a crime of passion, or whether Jimmy does this to protect the world from the monster Crake has become.

As Snowman, he reveals himself as a morally ambiguous man. He is a person of great sadness, yet he shoulders the responsibility put on him by both his mother and Crake. He will protect the Crakers, even with his own life.

Uncle En

Uncle En is the man who comes to Oryx's village to persuade the poor people to sell their children. He does not treat the children unkindly, according to Oryx, but he does initiate them into the child sex trade.

Uncle Pete

Uncle Pete is Crake's mother's boyfriend, who lives with her and Crake after Crake's father dies. He has a stash of skunkweed, another name for marijuana, and he also has passwords for pornographic Web sites. He dies of a virulent disease, and the implication is that Crake has killed him.

Motherhood

While it might seem strange to think about motherhood as a theme in *Oryx and Crake* in that the mothers are largely absent, their very absence forms a thematic thread. Indeed, this thread continues back to Atwood's 1985 novel *The Handmaid's Tale*. In this novel, the narrator Offred's mother is an environmental activist who initially appears only in Offred's memory; her mother has disappeared. Later, Offred discovers that her mother has been arrested and shipped off to the interior part of the country to clean up toxic wastes. She finds this out when she sees her mother in a newsreel film.

In *Oryx and Crake*, Jimmy's mother seems absent even before she finally leaves the family. Her unhappiness with her marriage and with the corporation for which she and her husband work leads her to feeling trapped and powerless. She grows distant from both her husband and her son. When she finally decides to leave, it becomes clear that she really *was* trapped. She must fake a visit to a dentist for a root canal in order to leave the compound.

While her commitment to her beliefs might be seen as admirable in other circumstances, in *Oryx and Crake*, her decision to leave comes across as selfish and destructive to her son. As Shuli Barzilai notes in an article appearing in *Critique*, "She does not love him enough to put him before her own needs and desires. She abandons Jimmy for a cause … that she ardently embraces." Worse, she takes away Jimmy's rakunk, a decision she makes on the basis of her own firmly held beliefs rather than Jimmy's feelings.

In the years that follow, she sends postcards to Jimmy, unsigned and sent from unknown locations. Rather than establishing a motherly presence, however, the postcards merely underscore her absence.

Crake's mother is also a shadowy figure. There are not many references to her in the story, only the comment that she likes Jimmy and that she began living with Uncle Pete, her boyfriend, after Crake's father died. Much later in the story, Crake reveals that his father died not from simply falling off a bridge but because he was pushed. Although not explicitly stated, the implication is that Crake's mother had some part in the assassination; she either plotted against him or did nothing to save him. When she dies a particularly gruesome death, the victim of a virus that dissolves her, there is the additional implication that Crake may have orchestrated her death. In any event, the nature of the virus causes her to literally disappear, again pointing to her absence as a mother figure.

Finally, Oryx's mother, in desperate circumstances, chooses to sell her children. Although she may believe that she is ensuring their survival, in reality, she has condemned them to lives devoid of love and nurturance. Indeed, this mother turns her own children into a commodity, using them as a means of exchange.

Topics for Further Study

- In *Oryx and Crake*, Atwood sets her story in a time in the near future, when global warming has changed the climate significantly. Using recent, credible sources on the Internet and in your library, research global warming. What do scientists predict will happen within the next twenty years? Within the next century? Locate specific references to the weather in *Oryx and Crake*. Does her book seem to follow scientific predictions? Write a researched-based essay reporting your findings about the possibility of the events Atwood imagines actually happening. Be sure to cite your sources.

- South African writer Lauren Beukes's *Moxyland* (2008) is set in Cape Town, South Africa, in the near future. Corporations are powerful, disease epidemics run rampant, and terrorist attacks are always a threat. Read *Moxyland* with a group of your peers. How is Beukes's vision of the future similar to or different from Atwood's? With your small group, prepare an imaginary newscast originating either in the world of *Oryx and Crake* or in Moxyland, reporting on a major news event. Record your newscast and post it to YouTube for your classmates to view and critique.

- Create an online, interactive poster using Glogster (http://www.glogster.com) that captures the essence of *Oryx and Crake*. To effectively complete the task, you should address the themes, characters, and contexts of the book. Upload your poster to your Web page.

- *Oryx and Crake* comments at length on genetic engineering. Research the topic of genetic engineering by consulting reputable Web sites, books, and journal articles. What are the limits of genetic engineering at present? What kinds of gene splicing are scientists currently undertaking? Do you think genetic engineering will help people or harm people? With a group of your classmates, prepare a debate on the topic, arguing for or against unlimited genetic research and engineering.

- Language is an important theme for Atwood in all of her novels. In *Oryx and Crake*, she creates Jimmy as someone who loves language and who collects words that are nearing extinction. Make a list of these words and look up their definitions. Choose ten words and do a ten-minute free writing session on each. Using Wordle (http://www.wordle.net), paste in your list of words and your free writing and make a word cloud. Experiment with color, font, size, and orientation. Print and post your word cloud in your classroom.

- Like *Oryx and Crake*, M. T. Anderson's young-adult novel *Feed* (2004) satirizes consumerism and the intrusion of corporations into the lives of its characters. Read *Feed* and *Oryx and Crake* and identify specific examples from contemporary culture that Anderson and Atwood satirize. With a group of your peers, create a television commercial that satirizes some aspect of contemporary culture. Record the commercial and upload it to YouTube for viewing by your classmates. Write a short essay explaining why you chose the example you did and how your commercial satisfies the definition of satire.

In these instances, Atwood has created mothers who behave badly and who do not nurture their offspring. Lorrie Moore, writing in the *New Yorker*, suggests one remaining mother thematically underpinning the novel: "The ur-mother in *Oryx and Crake* is, of course, Mother Nature herself—captured, tortured, and mocked, in classic gothic fashion, but elusive and indestructible, in her way." Atwood's Mother Nature is not a nurturing, loving force, providing sustenance for her children, but rather a tortured, vengeful, violent force that must be reckoned with.

Science

Science is an important thematic concern, and

it is evident reading the acknowledgment page that Atwood spent significant time researching the current state of knowledge in bioengineering. Moreover, Atwood grew up in a household of scientists. As Earl G. Ingersoll writes in an article appearing in *Extrapolation*, she was obliged to "'read up on' the popularized science of Stephen Jay Gould and others to have some background for dinner-table conversation." For *Oryx and Crake*, Atwood did not have to invent anything new for the science represented in the novel. Rather, Atwood maintains that "the science in *Oryx and Crake* represents a mere extension of present knowledge in genetic engineering," according to Ingersoll. Thus, both her research and her background have led her to speculate about what happens when the implications of new scientific discoveries are pushed to extremes.

For Atwood, this sometimes involves satire, such as her description of ChickieNobs, the chickens grown with multiple legs or breasts for use in the fast food industry. As disgusting as the sight of these creatures is for Jimmy, later in the book he eats ChickieNobs. In this case, Atwood highlights how humans will use the products of science while conveniently ignoring the means through which those products have been attained.

Atwood also satirizes genetic scientists at OrganInc Farms. This group engages in a competition called "Create a Species" for no other reason than the competition. In this instance, the scientists have lost reverence for life; they essentially are joking around with the building blocks of life, the DNA sequencing of various species. They do it simply because they can. Ironically, the creatures the scientists create in jest become feral and dangerous when they escape the confines of the laboratory.

Atwood thematically attacks the unholy marriage of science and profit. It does not take much digging to find examples of this in the real world. For example, food giant Nestlé acquired Jenny Craig, a weight loss company, in 2006, according to Andrew Ross Sorkin, writing in the *New York Times*. The company also owns the Lean Cuisine product line. At the same time, Nestlé also manufactures Digiorno Pizza, Hot Pockets, a wide assortment of candy lines, and Häagen-Dazs ice cream. Thus, in the pursuit of profit, Nestlé produces products that increase obesity, as well as products that supposedly combat obesity. Consumers who purchase and consume too much candy and ice cream can then purchase and consume diet products. The cycle ensures that the company that produces both will always turn a profit. The world of *Oryx and Crake* pushes this cycle to the extreme, with science-driven food and pharmaceutical companies interested only in the bottom line.

While it is possible to view some of the scientific work in *Oryx and Crake* as rooted in a sincere desire to help humankind by providing medicine and organs for transplant, the novel also shows the dark underbelly of the pharmaceutical industry. With the BlyssPluss pill, the industry not only creates a product for profit that sells like wildfire but it also creates the conditions for the destruction of all humankind.

Although science in *Oryx and Crake* is often shown in a negative light, Atwood herself does not see science as bad in and of itself. In an interview with Atwood appearing on the Random House *Oryx and Crake* Web site, Atwood states,

> Please don't make the mistake of thinking that *Oryx and Crake* is anti-science. Science is a way of knowing, and a tool. Like all ways of knowing and tools, it can be turned to bad uses. But it is not in itself bad. Like electricity, it's neutral.

The message of *Oryx and Crake*, then, is this: science divorced from ethics and morality is a dangerous tool, one that can lead to places no human ever wants to go.

Bildungsroman

A *bildungsroman* is a type of story that traces the moral and psychological growth of a central character from childhood to adulthood. In English, the form is often referred to as a coming-of-age-story. The word *bildung* means formation, and throughout a bildungsroman, the protagonist faces challenges and finds teachers who help form his or her character. *Star Wars* offers a familiar example: young Luke Skywalker grows from a young man who knows nothing of the outside world to become a Jedi knight, as a result of difficult challenges and circumstances. Along the way, his mentor Obi-Wan Kenobi and his teacher Yoda help him. Viewers watch as Luke undergoes the process of spiritual, psychological, physical, and emotional formation and grows into a man worthy of respect.

Although not as obviously, *Oryx and Crake* also functions as an example of the genre. As Barzilai points out, the fractured chronology of the story and the constant shifting from present to past hide the straightforward story of growth one expects to find in a bildungsroman. However, when the parts of the story are reordered sequentially, according to Barzilai, "what emerges is the story of the constitution of a twenty-first century (male) subject whose primary caretakers and educators include the electronic media: the Internet, video games, and television."

The picture of young Jimmy that first emerges is that of a child who does not understand the world nor himself. He hungers for the attention of his parents, but they are so wrapped up in their own problems that they ignore him. This neglect contributes to the adult Jimmy becomes, someone who is unable to establish intimate relationships. When Jimmy's mother leaves, he feels deserted. From this point on, he finds it difficult to trust anyone.

Later, readers discover that Jimmy has little ambition and does not apply himself to his studies. Although he is older, he has not grown much. He still takes the easy way and prefers to immerse himself in video games rather than educate himself about the world. Still later, when he meets Oryx and falls in love with her, he betrays his best friend by having an affair with her. This would not appear to be growth; however, his relationship with Oryx is formative. Through his love for her and through her simple acceptance of life, he begins to stop seeing himself as a victim.

Jimmy is a late bloomer. Little that has happened during the course of the novel suggests that he will have the strength of character to be completely responsible for the Crakers. Yet when civilization ends, Jimmy does as Crake has asked him: he does not let the Crakers down. He steps into a role he does not want and performs it to the best of his ability. By the end of the story, it appears that he is willing to risk his life to protect the Crakers.

Menippean Satire

A Menippean satire is a long prose work that attacks social structures and attitudes. Named after the Greek cynic Menippus, the form has a long literary history that includes works such as Jonathan Swift's *Gulliver's Travels*, Voltaire's *Candide*, and Lewis Carroll's *Alice in Wonderland*. Chris Baldick, writing in *The Oxford Dictionary of Literary Terms*, notes that Menippean satire often includes "miscellaneous contents" and "displays of curious erudition."

Oryx and Crake is clearly satire when considered in these terms. In the first place, Atwood chooses a wide variety of content to satirize in her book: climate change and global warming, bioengineering, commercialization of life, the loss of government and the rise of corporations, security fears, terrorism, the commodification of sex, and the extinction of many life forms, among others. As she ranges among these topics, Atwood displays erudition (that is, educated mastery of a topic) beyond what a reader might expect in a novel. Her erudition gives her the authority to satirize. In each of these topics, Atwood starts with what is already present in contemporary life and then extrapolates what might happen in these areas in the future. For example, scientists warn that global warming will cause serious climate change and unsettling weather conditions in the future if humans do not stop burning fossil fuels. Atwood guesses the humans will neither limit their consumption of gas nor cease to burn coal, and so when she projects the global warming trend into the future, she sees a world where the East Coast of the United States is under water, the Midwest and West are dry and drought-stricken, and storms rage through temperate latitudes every afternoon. Likewise, she knows that scientists have concerns about the destruction of the ozone layer (the atmospheric layer that protects the Earth from dangerous radiation) due to the use of fluorocarbons. She guesses that the trend will continue, and so she creates a future where radiation from the sun is deadly to humans, although not to Crakers.

Further, Brian Lee, in *The Routledge Dictionary of Literary Terms*, quotes literary critic Northrup Frye on satire: "Satire demands at least a token fantasy, a content which the reader recognizes as grotesque, and at least an implicit moral standard." *Oryx and Crake* fulfills this requirement. The entire book is fantasy. Although it is possible to see Atwood's future firmly rooted in the present, she pushes the implication of those roots to their extreme, in order to shock and amuse her readers. For example, in present-day society, the fast food industry utilizes vast quantities of chicken meat. Bioengineering has already created poultry with huge breasts in order to increase the amount of white meat (such as the Honeysuckle White brand of turkey). Atwood pushes this trend into the future and posits the bioengineering of chickens that have no heads, beaks, or eyes. These chickens grow multiple breasts or drumsticks. The product will find its way into the fast food industry as ChickieNobs. Although Jimmy is disgusted, later in the book, ChickieNobs has become part of everyday life, and Jimmy himself eats them.

ChickieNobs also show Atwood's implicit moral standard regarding food and the humane treatment of animals. By portraying fast food and bioengineering at their most grotesque, she implies that both are morally wrong when they create inferior products that require the inhumane treatment of animals.

Bioterrorism

The plot of *Oryx and Crake* revolves around an event that is not explained or made clear until late in the book, yet every other thing that happens in the novel pushes the plot toward the dreadful moment when Crake, in an unthinkable example of bioterrorism, unleashes a terrible plague on the world, a plague that destroys human civilization.

It is perhaps not a surprise the bioterrorism would be at the core of Atwood's novel; in her speculative fiction, Atwood often appears to be prophetic. She began writing *Oryx and Crake* in about 2001, after having "dreamed" the book while visiting Australia. Suddenly, it was September 11, 2001: two planes flew into the World Trade Center in New York, another hit the Pentagon in Washington, DC, and a fourth plane, headed to Washington, crashed in rural Pennsylvania when passengers overpowered the terrorists who had killed the flight crew.

Then, within weeks, letters and packages containing a deadly weaponized form of the anthrax bacterium were sent through the United States mail. In a 2008 briefing, the Federal Bureau of Investigation called the anthrax scare "the worst case of bioterrorism in U.S. history." Although only five people died and seventeen were sickened, according to the FBI, the scare caused panic and mayhem in a nation already demoralized by the September 11 attacks. Further, the anthrax investigation cost the country millions of dollars and worker-hours over the next decade.

In the 2008 briefing, the FBI and Department of Justice attributed the anthrax attacks to one man, Dr. Bruce Ivins, who committed suicide before charges could be leveled against him. According to National Public Radio's David Kestenbaum, Ivins worked as a microbiologist for over thirty years at the Army's biodefense laboratory at Fort Detrick, in Maryland.

In an interview appearing on Random House's *Oryx and Crake* Web page, Atwood said that she did not change the plot after the events of September and October 2001, but she almost gave up writing the book. "Real life was getting creepily too close to my inventions—not so much the Twin Towers as the anthrax scare. … The main object of these kinds of actions is to sow panic and dismay."

SARS

While the anthrax scare was a terrorist attack, its scope was limited. Potentially more dangerous was the 2002–2003 outbreak of a virus causing severe acute respiratory syndrome (SARS). This was a naturally occurring outbreak, not bioterrorism. However, the rapidity with which the disease spread and the high rate of infection associated with the disease struck fear into both the medical community and the general population. Worldwide, according to the U.S. Centers for Disease Control (CDC), 8,098 people became ill with SARS, and 774 people died between November 2002 and July 2003. Like the epidemic in *Oryx and Crake*, SARS broke out around the world almost simultaneously. The CDC reports that there were cases in more than two dozen countries.

Forty-four people died in Toronto, Ontario, Canada, of SARS during this period, and the city was in virtual lockdown. The Canadian Broadcasting Corporation (CBC), in an April 22, 2004 news story on *CBC News Online*, reported that Ontario Justice Archie Campbell "observed that Ontario's health system had been unable to manage the crisis. ... The province's medical infrastructure was pushed to its limits and the region's hospitality industry was also paralyzed by the outbreak."

SARS brought to light the serious social disruption that takes place in an epidemic, even a small one. Thus, it does not take a very great stretch of the imagination to imagine a worldwide epidemic or plague bringing down all of human civilization.

Global Warming

Throughout *Oryx and Crake*, readers see evidence that the Earth's climate is in real trouble, even before the day the Crake unleashes the virus. In creating her setting, Atwood drew on scientific information regarding global warming and climate change available in the early 2000s. She imagined that all of the scientists' predictions were accurate, and accordingly created an environment that would reflect those predictions.

The statistics available to Atwood during the writing of *Oryx and Crake* regarding global warming were frightening. Moreover, those predictions have remained largely the same since the turn of the twenty-first century.

Holli Riebeek, writing in NASA's *Earth Observatory*, summarizes the effects, stating, "For most places, global warming will result in more frequent hot days and fewer cool days. … Longer, more intense heat waves will become more common. Storms, floods, and droughts will generally be more severe." This, in turn, will lead to changes in agriculture and food production.

In addition, global warming will cause sea levels to rise, potentially inundating coastal areas. In *Oryx and Crake*, this has already happened along the East Coast of the United States. As sea levels rise, not only will farmlands be flooded but they will be flooded with salty seawater that kills any crops and prevents further farming of the land. Again, food shortages could result.

Scientists also predict that infectious diseases will increase. For example, mosquitoes that carry malaria are already moving north-ward from tropical areas. It is possible that malaria will become a serious health risk in the southern United States in decades to come.

These changes will have a serious impact on

all life on earth. Because all life is intertwined, a change in one ecosystem necessarily has an impact on others. Atwood's vision of the future grows directly out of present-day scientific research.

Critical Overview

With *Oryx and Crake*, Atwood returned to the genre of speculative fiction she first explored in *The Handmaid's Tale*. The novel was reviewed widely, provoking discussion and debate and gaining the book a wide readership. A critical success, the novel was shortlisted for the Booker Prize in 2003.

Contemporary reviews were generally very favorable. For example, in a review appearing in *Américas*, critic Barbara Mujica writes, "Replete with dark humor, Margaret Atwood's brilliantly crafted new novel is magnificently entertaining." Likewise, short story author Moore, writing in the *New Yorker*, calls *Oryx and Crake* a "towering and intrepid" novel.

Some critics view *Oryx and Crake* as a novel that should be noted for its ideas, rather than for its plot or action. Tom Wilhelmus, writing in *Hudson Review*, argues that what is "most interesting" about the novel "is not the rather obvious machinery of the plot but rather the archaeological insight Atwood brings to life today as she looks back on it from the future." In contrast, well-known literary scholar Elaine Showalter sees the novel as one of action and suspense. Writing in the *London Review of Books*, Showalter calls *Oryx and Crake* "a highly cinematic adventure story of daring and survival." Further, she contrasts the novel to Atwood's earlier works in which the writer "never emphasised action."

Not all contemporary reviewers were as positive about *Oryx and Crake*. Hugo Barnacle, for example, writing in *New Statesman*, suggests that Atwood's plot repeats that of a Tom Clancy novel, and although Atwood's version is "just as readable, and more elegantly written" than Clancy's novel, *Oryx and Crake* nonetheless "contrives to be at once sillier and less funny."

In the years since the publication of the novel, literary scholars have analyzed *Oryx and Crake* in a variety of ways. In an article in *Science Fiction Studies* comparing Oryx and Crake with William Gibson's *Pattern Recognition* and Greg Egan's *Schild's Ladder*, Veronica Hollinger reads *Oryx and Crake* as "a satire about the catastrophic potential of increasingly commodified technoscience." She argues, "Of these three novels, Atwood's is the most concerned to encourage something like conventional political action on the part of its readers."

Shari Evans, writing in *Femspec*, agrees: "The desire to warn contemporary society seems to be the impetus behind each of Atwood's speculative forays, *The Handmaid's Tale* and *Oryx and Crake*." She also believes that Atwood's novel offers a small measure of hope. Through individual action, the slide toward dystopia can be stopped:

> Atwood's novel ... offers a glimpse of redemption through individual practice. This utopic hope—that

individual human decisions can begin to reverse the tide of dystopic disintegration—suggests that something as slight as an individual's ethical decision can alter the overwhelming cultural forces that inundate our lives.

The novel's conclusion, she contends, offers Snowman the chance to make an ethical decision, to not kill the other humans. Although this is an unsafe option, it is also "the right thing to do."

Ingersoll, writing in *Extrapolation*, on the other hand, focuses on the theme of survival in *Oryx and Crake*. He also offers a clear study of the contexts in which Atwood wrote the novel, showing that the novel should be read in connection not only to *The Handmaid's Tale* but also to other works of fiction, including *Frankenstein*, 1984, and *Brave New World*, among others. Similarly, in her book *Margaret Atwood*, Coral Ann Howells comments on the wide range of genres that Atwood uses in her novel: "dystopia, satire, wilderness survival narrative and castaway narrative, tragic romance triangle, and the quest to the Underworld."

Finally, many scholars use ecocriticism, the study of literature and the environment, to discuss *Oryx and Crake*. Heidi Slettedahl Macpherson, writing in *The Cambridge Introduction to Margaret Atwood*, notes that "the environmental concerns Atwood raised in *The Handmaid's Tale* are writ large in *Oryx and Crake*. ... She creates a world that valorizes science and lets scientists play God."

From Macpherson's perspective, Atwood's concern with the environment comes down to ethical choices; scientists must be held accountable. She argues, "[The novel] is based on present-day practices and the potential of scientists to deny the ethics of their acts. Atwood casts an artist's eye over this power, and asks us, the readers, to do the same."

What Do I Read Next?

- Nancy Farmer's young-adult novel *The House of the Scorpion* (2002) is a futuristic story set in a country called Opium, a land that was once Mexico. The protagonist, Matteo Alacrán, is a boy cloned from the DNA of El Patrón. Conceived in a Petri dish and incubated in a cow's womb, Matteo faces sinister characters and his own struggle to understand himself. The book won the 2002 National Book Award for Young People's Literature and was a 2003 Newberry Honor Book.

- In *The Year of the Flood* (2009), Atwood returns to the same setting as *Oryx and Crake*, in the days immediately before and after the catastrophe. Many of the same characters populate both novels.

- Nathalie Cooke's *Margaret Atwood: A Biography* (1998) remains the standard Atwood biography. Cooke's later book, *Margaret Atwood: A Critical Companion* (2004), provides not only biographical detail but also a critical overview of all Atwood's major works through *The Blind Assassin*.

- *Brave New World*, written by Aldous Huxley in 1931 and published in 1932, is often noted as an influence on Atwood's *Oryx and Crake*. Like Atwood, Huxley provides a frightening and satiric vision of the future that addresses many of the pressing issues of his own time.

- *Opposing Viewpoints: Genetic Engineering*, edited by David M. Haugen in 2009, is a collection of articles debating the pros and cons of genetic engineering for a young-adult audience.

- Susan Beth Pfeffer's *Life As We Knew It* (2008) is a coming-of-age story featuring high school student Miranda, who must contend with the after-effects of a huge meteor hitting the moon, pushing it off its axis, and causing earthquakes and tsunamis on Earth.

- Atwood chooses lines from Jonathan Swift's *Gulliver's Travels* as an epigraph to *Oryx and Crake*, and many critics have cited the influence of this book on Atwood's speculative fiction. Although written in 1726, *Gulliver's Travels* remains a classic of social satire.

- Climate scientists Michael E. Mann and Lee R. Klump collaborated on the 2008 book *Dire Predictions: Understanding Global Warming*, which explains the findings of the Intergovernmental Panel on Climate Change in lucid prose designed for the lay reader. The book contains many photos, charts, illustrations, and artwork.

Hacking Darwin
Jamie Metzl

Sources

"Anthrax Investigation: Closing a Chapter," in *Federal Bureau of Investigation*, August 6, 2008, http://www.fbi.gov/news/stories/2008/august/amerit (accessed July 15, 2011).

Atwood, Margaret, "*The Handmaid's Tale and Oryx and Crake* in Context," *inPMLA*, Vol. 119, No. 3, May 2004, pp. 513–17.

_____, *Oryx and Crake*, Doubleday, 2003.

_____, *Survival: A Thematic Guide to Canadian Literature*, 3rd ed., McClellan & Stewart, 2004, p. 42.

"Author Q & A," Random House Web site, http://www.randomhouse.com/acmart/catalog/displa isbn=9780739304082&view=qa (accessed July 15, 2011).

Baldick, Chris, "Menippean Satire," in *The Oxford Dictionary of Literary Terms*, 3rd ed., Oxford University Press, 2008, p. 202.

Barnacle, Hugo, "The End Is Nigh," in *New Statesman*, Vol. 132, No. 4638, May 19, 2003, p. 50.

Barzilai, Shuli, "'Tell My Story': Remembrance and Revenge in Atwood's *Oryx and Crake* and Shakespeare's *Hamlet*," in *Critique*, Vol. 50, No. 1, Fall 2008, pp. 87–110.

"Biography," in *Margaret Atwood Home Page*,

http://www.margaretatwood.ca/bio.php (accessed July 5, 2011).

Evans, Shari, "'Not Unmarked': From Themed Space to a Feminist Ethics of Engagement in Atwood's *Oryx and Crake*," in *Femspec*, Vol. 10, No. 2, 2010, pp. 35–58.

"Fact Sheet: Basic Information about SARS," in *Severe Acute Respiratory Syndrome*, Centers for Disease Control and Prevention, May 3, 2005, http://www.cdc.gov/ncidod/sars/factsheet.htm (accessed July 15, 2011).

Hollinger, Veronica, "Stories about the Future: From Patterns of Expectation to Pattern Recognition," in *Science Fiction Studies*, Vol. 33, No. 3, November 2006, pp. 452–72.

Howells, Coral Ann, *Margaret Atwood*, 2nd ed., Palgrave McMillan, 2005, pp. 1–19, 170–91.

Ingersoll, Earl G., "Survival in Margaret Atwood's Novel *Oryx and Crake*," in *Extrapolation*, Vol. 45, No. 2, June 22, 2004, pp. 162–75.

Kestenbaum, David, "Who Was Bruce Ivins?" in *All Things Considered*, National Public Radio, August 1, 2008, http://www.npr.org/templates/story/story.php?storyId=93194941 (accessed July 15, 2011).

Lee, Brian, "Satire," in *The Routledge Dictionary of Literary Terms*, edited by Peter Childs and Roger Fowler, Routledge, 2006, p. 211.

Macpherson, Heidi Slettedahl, *The Cambridge Introduction to Margaret Atwood*, Cambridge

University Press, 2010, pp. 1–10, 78–82.

Moore, Lorrie, "Bioperversity," in *New Yorker*, Vol. 79, No. 12, May 19, 2003, p. 88.

Mujica, Barbara, "Of Fantastic Futures and Imagined Pasts," in *Américas*, Vol. 55, No. 5, September/October 2003, p. 55.

Posner, Richard, "The End Is Near," in *New Republic*, Vol. 229, No. 12, September 22, 2003, pp. 31–36.

Riebeek, Holli, "Global Warming," in *Earth Observatory*, National Aeronautic and Space Administration, June 3, 2010, http://earthobservatory.nasa.gov/Features/GlobalWai (accessed July 24, 2011).

"Severe Acute Respiratory Syndrome," in *CBC News Online*, April 22, 2004, http://www.cbc.ca/news/background/sars (accessed July 15, 2011).

Showalter, Elaine, "The Snowman Cometh," in *London Review of Books*, Vol. 25, No. 14, July 24, 2003, p. 35.

Sorkin, Andrew Ross, "Nestlé to Buy Jenny Craig, Betting Diets Are on Rise," in *New York Times*, June 19, 2006, http://www.nytimes.com/2006/06/19/business/world (accessed July 20, 2011).

Thompson, Lee Briscoe, "Margaret Atwood," in *Dictionary of Literary Biography*, Vol. 251, *Canadian Fantasy and Science Fiction Writers*, edited by Douglas Ivison, The Gale Group, 2002, pp. 11–21.

Wilhelmus, Tom, "Next," in *Hudson Review*, Vol. 57, No. 1, Spring 2004, pp. 133–40.

Further Reading

Berger, James Hank, *After the End: Representations of Post-Apocalypse*, University of Minnesota Press, 1999.

> Berger examines artistic, literary, and cinematic works that portray postapocalyptic Earth. He notes the features of contemporary culture that influence these works, as well as the way that postapocalyptic representation affects culture.

Ingersoll, Earl G., ed., *Waltzing Again: New and Selected Conversations with Margaret Atwood*, Ontario Review Press, 2006.

> Ingersoll presents twenty-one interviews with Atwood, held from 1972 to 2006, including a 1972 interview with Atwood's partner Graeme Gibson. Atwood's intelligence and wit are clearly evident throughout.

Sullivan, Rosemary, *The Red Shoes: Margaret Atwood Starting Out*, HarperCollins, 1998.

> Sullivan's biography provides details about Atwood's early years in the 1940s, 1950s, and 1960s, concluding in the early 1970s.

Wilson, E. O., *The Future of Life*, Knopf, 2002.

Atwood suggests in an interview on the *Oryx and Crake* page at the Random House Web site that if readers were to read just one additional book, it should be this one by famed Harvard biologist E. O. Wilson. The book summarizes the condition of the earth at present, as well as the chances for survival of the human race.

Wynn-Davies, Marion, *Margaret Atwood*, Writers and Their Work series, Northcote House Publishers, 2010.

Wynn-Davies presents a critical study of Atwood, examining the connections among Atwood's work and feminism, multiculturalism, terrorism, ecology, and global warming.

Suggested Search Terms

Margaret Atwood

Oryx and Crake

Margaret Atwood AND Oryx and Crake

The Handmaid's Tale AND Atwood

Year of the Flood AND Atwood

postapocalypse

speculative fiction

genetic engineering

science fiction AND Margaret Atwood

Menippean satire

quest story

survival

Canadian writers